Rusty Edwards
As Sunshine to a Garden

Hymns and Songs

Augsburg Fortress
Minneapolis

AS SUNSHINE TO A GARDEN
Hymns and Songs
Rusty Edwards

Copyright © 1999 Augsburg Fortress. All rights reserved.

Except for brief quotations in critical articles or reviews, no part of this book may be reproduced in any manner without prior written permission from the publisher or from the other copyright holders. Permission requests should be directed to: Permissions, Augsburg Fortress, P.O. Box 1209, Minneapolis, MN 55440-1209, USA; fax line: 1-612-330-3252; e-mail: copyright@augsburgfortress.org

The paper used in this publication meets the minimum requirements of American National Standard for Information Sciences—Permanence of Paper for Printed Materials, ANSI Z329.48-1984.

Manufactured in the U.S.A.   ISBN 0-8066-5856-6

Contents

Foreword	p. 4
Acknowledgments	5

Hymns and songs #1–46

Indexes

Topics and themes	p. 60
Scripture references	62
Tunes—alphabetical	63
Tunes—metrical	63
Contributors and sources	64
First lines and titles	64

Foreword

Rusty Edwards writes hymns of faith while watching sunsets, blowing winds, rain, and sun shining on gardens. He sees in God's world a language for music of faith, and hymns are born.

More than fifteen years ago, Rusty was my student. Following major surgery after I became ill that first year, I was brought to my room. There on the floor with his guitar, playing poems from my recent book, was Rusty—minstrel, healer, gentle singer. I could see rhyme and meter and hope in his face. It is still so with Rusty and these songs—songs meant to grow, to abide, to nurture the human spirit.

In the seventeenth century Paul Gerhardt wrote many hymns in difficult times to keep his congregation in faith. Rusty's songs have the same purpose. He hopes his songs will endure for generations and dwell long in singers' hearts. He does not want good songs to disappear.

Rusty does not walk solo on his musical journey; he is a collaborator, songwriter, and friend in community. He connects with others who offer texts, add tunes, create compositions. His music is meant for friends, for others, for you. It is all meant to glorify God.

As Sunshine to a Garden offers forty-six songs; mostly new, a few previously published, all created by this young pastor-poet-songwriter. These new songs are meant to become old friends, to be committed to memory and passed on to others. Many of the songs echo scripture, their words touchstones of faith that will sing themselves into minds and hearts.

Here are songs within a spiritual tradition worth inheriting. They are an inheritance for his children and for generations to come, a legacy of music his children and ours will sing and want to know by heart. The tunes are singable, the words make sense, and both give praise.

Some songs are personal, some communal. Rusty Edwards likes time alone, time with children, time with friends. He makes music, does ministry, loves family, plays tennis, goes boating, reaches mountaintops, listens and talks and walks with friends. Join this minstrel, singer of old and new psalms, as he walks and sings in God's garden of sunshine.

Herbert Brokering

Acknowledgments

My heartfelt thanks . . .

to God, from whom all blessings flow. May these songs glorify and magnify you.

to Lori, Benjamin, Ian, and my parents, for giving me the freedom to answer the call to hymn writing.

to Chick Corea, for twenty-five years of encouraging me to create with music, and to Herbert Brokering, for fifteen years of showing me the joy of creating with words.

to the authors and composers who through the years have blessed my work with theirs, and to the editors and publishers who have chosen to share these songs with a larger community. I'm especially grateful to those who contributed to hymns newly published in this volume: Susanne Bågenfelt, Skinnskatteburg, Sweden; Herbert Brokering, Minneapolis; Richard Drexler, Tampa; LaJuana Fiester, Marietta, Georgia; Jane Marshall, Dallas; Clayton J. Schmit, Durham, North Carolina; Linda Cable Shute, Roswell, Georgia; and my son Benjamin.

to Martin Seltz, Aaron Koelman, Suzanne Burke, and others at Augsburg Fortress for the care they have taken in the publishing of this collection.

finally to Kim Minick, whose love for family, friends, and the youth of my community inspired "The Garden Song." This one's for you!

Rusty Edwards
Advent 1999

1 As sunshine to a garden
The Garden Song

Text: Rusty Edwards
Music: THE GARDEN SONG, 7676; Susanne Bågenfelt

Be a searchlight 2

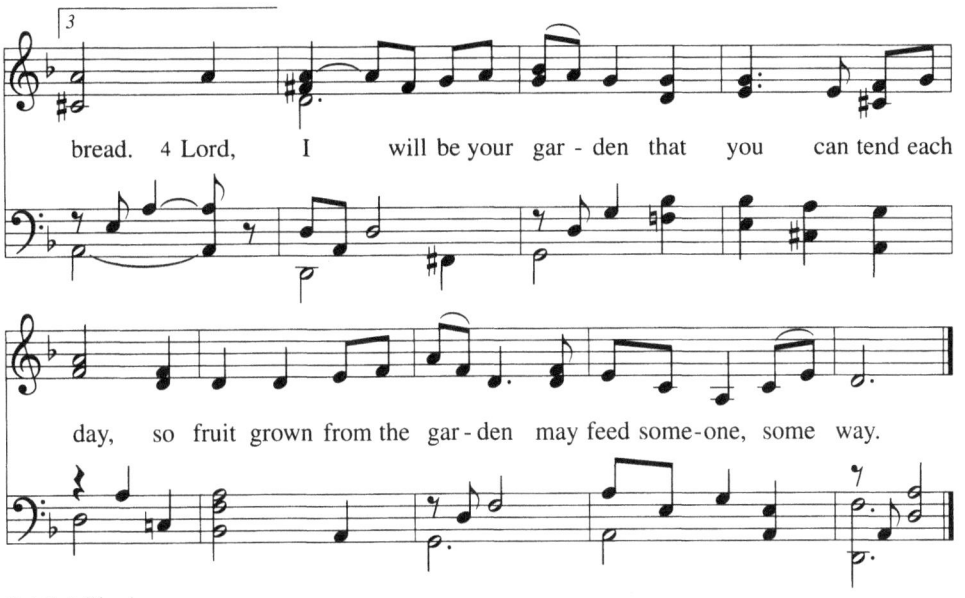

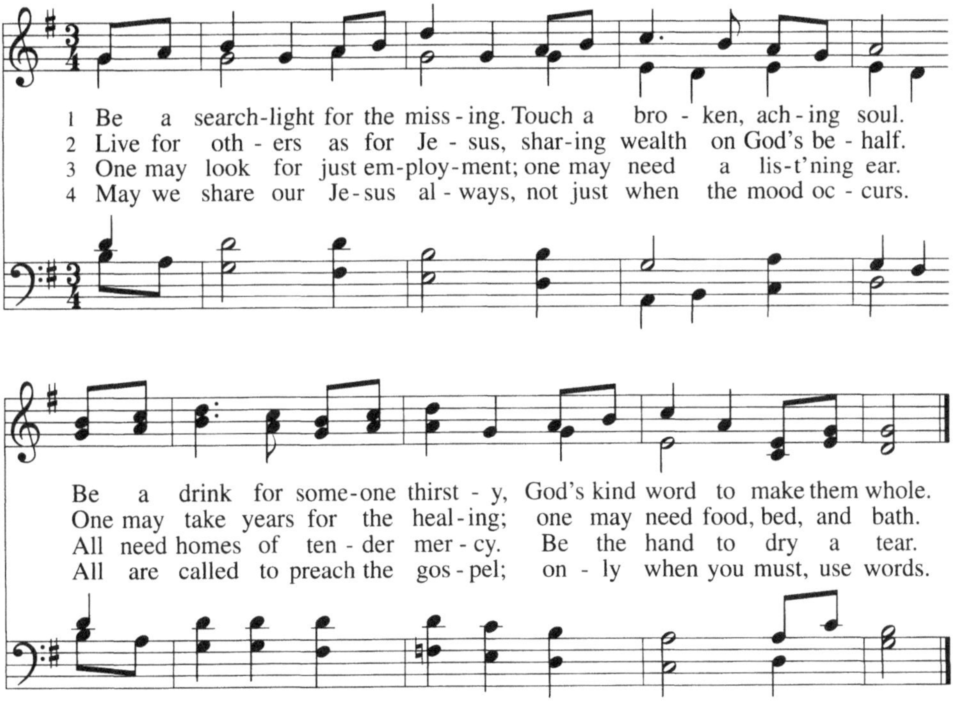

Text: Rusty Edwards
Music: BOB AND JERRY, 8787; Rusty Edwards

Bride and bridegroom

Refrain

Bride and bride-groom soon are ar-riv-ing! Wel-come to the day of the Lamb! Christ the bright morn-ing star is shin-ing as the most re-mark-a-ble gem.

Text: Rusty Edwards, based on Revelation 19:6–8
Music: LAMB'S WEDDING, 8 8 8 7 and refrain; Susanne Bågenfelt
© 1999 Augsburg Fortress

4 By grace we have been saved

1 By grace we have been saved through faith and not by keep-ing law.
2 For all have sinned and fall - en short. God's plan, not one o - beyed.
3 God gave to earth a per - fect love through Je - sus on the cross.
4 We know the wage of sin is death; thank God, we shall re - vive.
5 Set free, we now have peace with God. Sal - va - tion is se - cured.

God's saints be - lieved by what they heard and not by what they saw.
Christ has for all ful - filled the law. Be - lieve, con - fess, be saved.
While we were foes, Christ died for us. We gained by God's own loss.
For just as Je - sus rose a - gain, we too are made a - live.
How beau - ti - ful the feet of those who share this gos - pel word.

Refrain

Oh, how I love Je - sus! Oh, how I love Je - sus!

Oh, how I love Je - sus, be - cause he first loved me!

Text: Rusty Edwards, stanzas; Frederick Whitfield, refrain
Music: OH, HOW I LOVE JESUS, CM and refrain; North American traditional, arr. Rusty Edwards
Text © 1997 Selah Publishing Co.
Arr. © 1999 Augsburg Fortress

Cast your every care on me   5

Text: Rusty Edwards
Music: ONE LESS TEAR, 7777; Rusty Edwards
© 1999 Augsburg Fortress

6 Clap your hands! Shout for joy!

1 Clap your hands! Shout for joy! Awe-some is the Lord Most High. God shall reign o-ver all. Con-gre-ga-tion: heed the call.
2 Trum-pets sound. Laugh-ter rings. God as-cends a-bove all kings. God de-serves our best hymn, choirs that sing like cher-u-bim.
3 God will melt hearts of stone as we reach the ho-ly throne. Child-like sounds blend as one. Heav-en's cho-rus has be-gun.

Text: Rusty Edwards, based on Psalm 47
Music: KENNESAW MOUNTAIN, 6767; Linda Cable Shute
© 1999 Augsburg Fortress

Feed my lambs

For Mary Lou Mickey, in honor of her ministry at the Mary House, Bradenton, Florida

Text: Rusty Edwards
Music: MARY LOU, 9 11 9 11; Rusty Edwards
© 1999 Augsburg Fortress

9   For everything there is a time

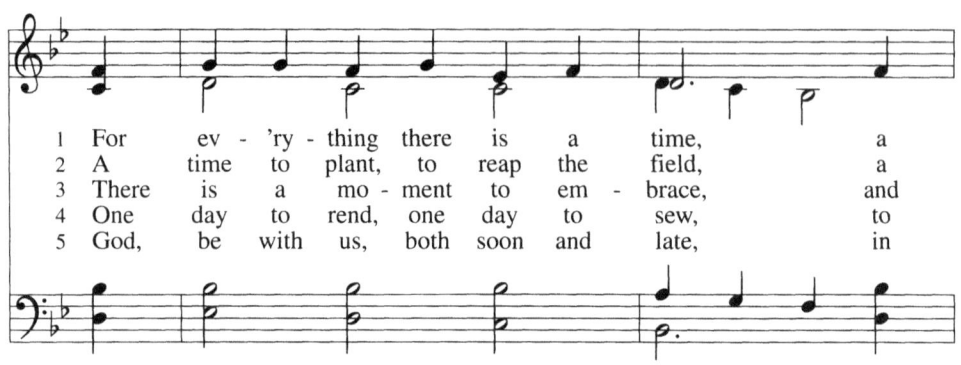

1. For ev-'ry-thing there is a time, a
2. A time to plant, to reap the field, a
3. There is a mo-ment to em-brace, and
4. One day to rend, one day to sew, to
5. God, be with us, both soon and late, in

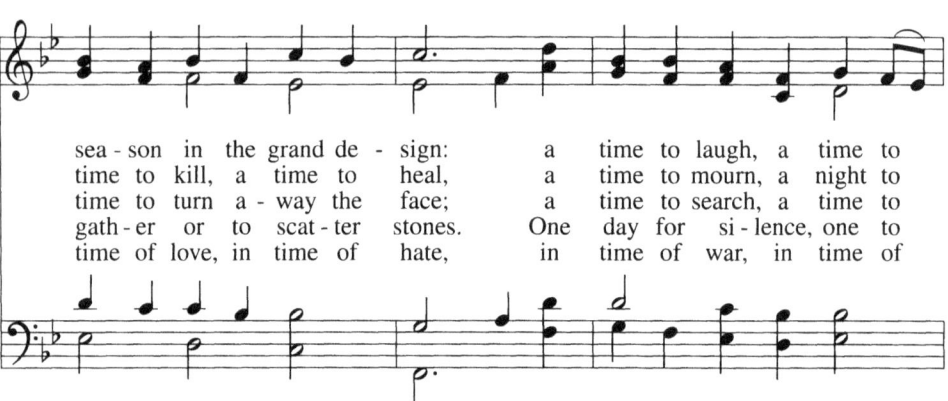

sea-son in the grand de-sign: a time to laugh, a time to
time to kill, a time to heal, a time to mourn, a night to
time to turn a-way the face; a time to search, a time to
gath-er or to scat-ter stones. One day for si-lence, one to
time of love, in time of hate, in time of war, in time of

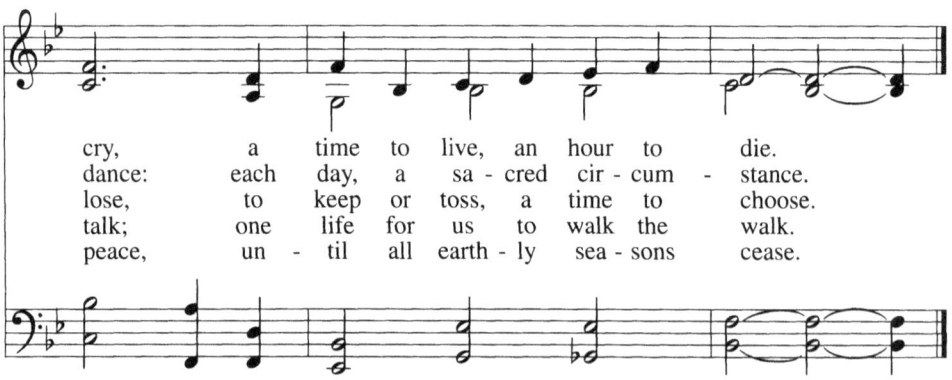

cry, a time to live, an hour to die.
dance: each day, a sa-cred cir-cum-stance.
lose, to keep or toss, a time to choose.
talk; one life for us to walk the walk.
peace, un-til all earth-ly sea-sons cease.

Text: Rusty Edwards, based on Ecclesiastes 3:1–8
Music: NARVESEN, LM; Rusty Edwards
© 1999 Augsburg Fortress

For God so loved the world

Refrain

For God so loved the world that God gave the on-ly Son,

that who-ev-er be-lieves in him shall have e-ter-nal life.

1 As Mo-ses lift-ed the ser-pent in the wil-der-ness,
2 For God sent Je-sus from heav-en to this world of ours
3 For sure-ly Je-sus has taught us that we must be born

Refrain

so the Son of God must be lift-ed that we may have life.
not to curse the world but to save us, that we may have life.
of the wa-ter and of the Spir-it, that we may have life.

Text: Rusty Edwards, based on John 3:5, 14-17
Music: THREE SIXTEEN, 8 5 9 5 and refrain; Rusty Edwards
© 1984 Hope Publishing Co.

13   God recycles, reconciles us

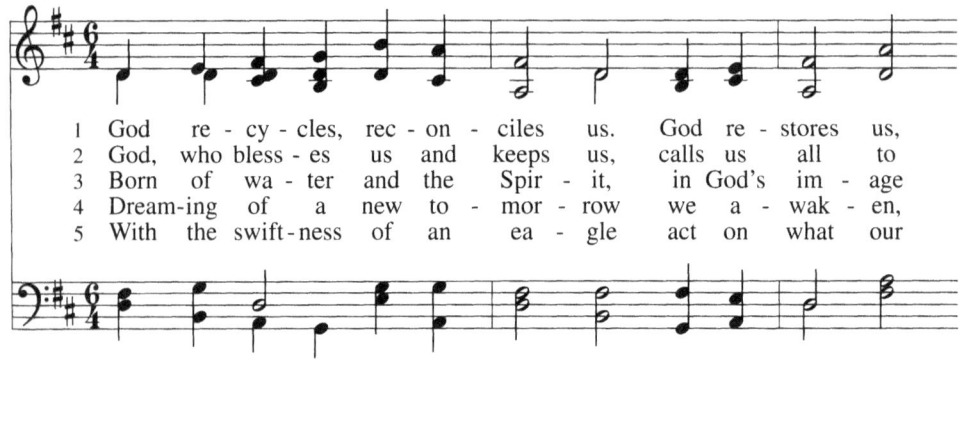

1 God re-cy-cles, rec-on-ciles us. God re-stores us,
2 God, who bless-es us and keeps us, calls us all to
3 Born of wa-ter and the Spir-it, in God's im-age
4 Dream-ing of a new to-mor-row we a-wak-en,
5 With the swift-ness of an ea-gle act on what our

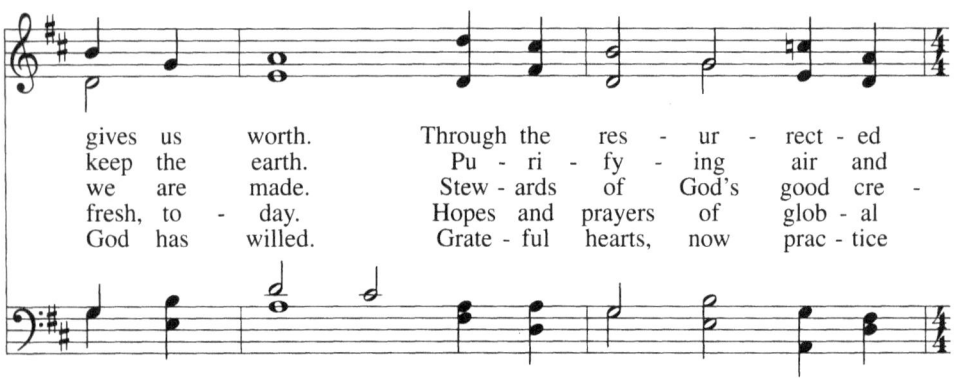

gives us worth. Through the res-ur-rect-ed
keep the earth. Pu-ri-fy-ing air and
we are made. Stew-ards of God's good cre-
fresh, to-day. Hopes and prayers of glob-al
God has willed. Grate-ful hearts, now prac-tice

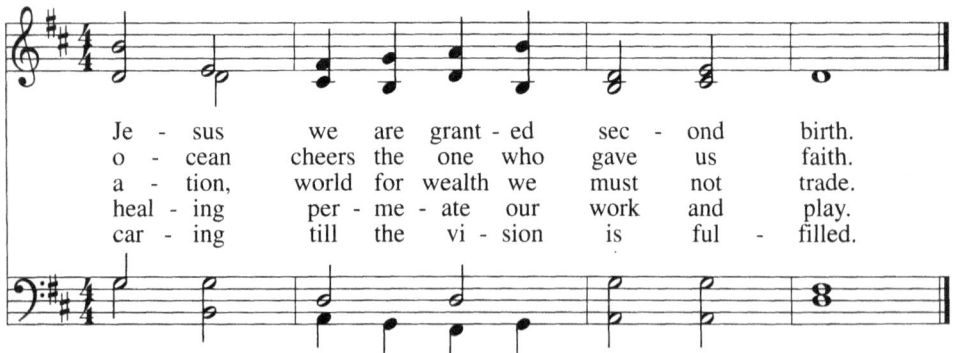

Je-sus we are grant-ed sec-ond birth.
o-cean cheers the one who gave us faith.
a-tion, world for wealth we must not trade.
heal-ing per-me-ate our work and play.
car-ing till the vi-sion is ful-filled.

Text: Rusty Edwards
Music: EARTH DAY HYMN, 8 7 8 7; Jane Marshall
© 1999 Augsburg Fortress

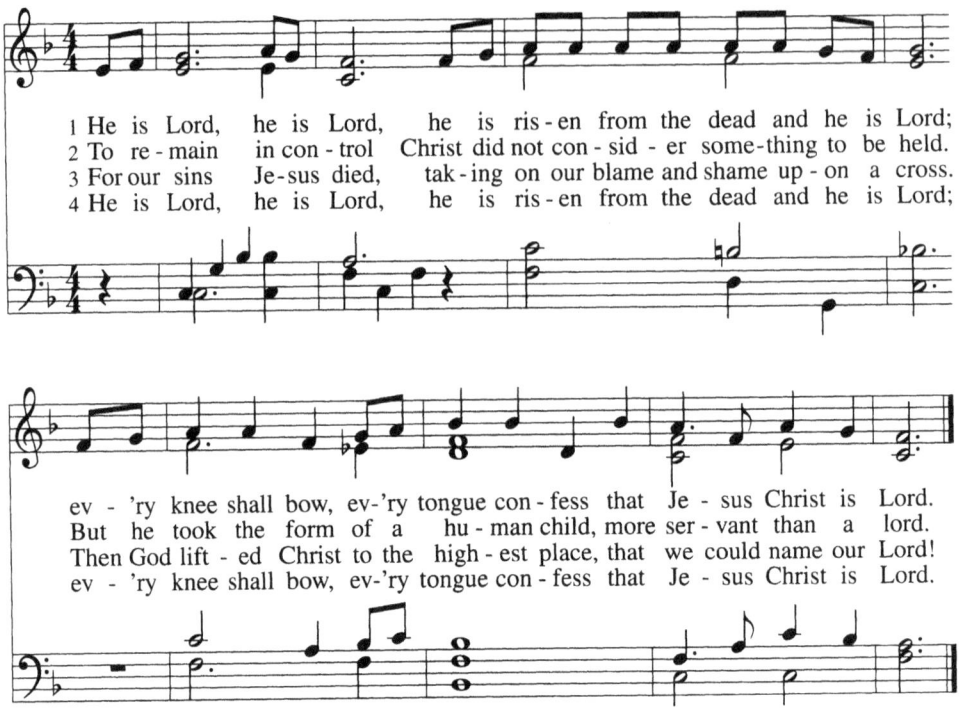

He is Lord

15

1 He is Lord, he is Lord, he is ris-en from the dead and he is Lord;
2 To re-main in con-trol Christ did not con-sid-er some-thing to be held.
3 For our sins Je-sus died, tak-ing on our blame and shame up-on a cross.
4 He is Lord, he is Lord, he is ris-en from the dead and he is Lord;

ev-'ry knee shall bow, ev-'ry tongue con-fess that Je-sus Christ is Lord.
But he took the form of a hu-man child, more ser-vant than a lord.
Then God lift-ed Christ to the high-est place, that we could name our Lord!
ev-'ry knee shall bow, ev-'ry tongue con-fess that Je-sus Christ is Lord.

Text: traditional, sts. 1 and 4; Rusty Edwards, sts. 2–3; based on Philippians 2:6-11
Music: HE IS LORD, 6 11 11 10 6; traditional
Text sts. 2–3 © 1999 Augsburg Fortress

Heal this old heart   16

1. Heal this old heart; it is breaking. Make it new, Lord, spirit waking.
2. Lord, have mercy, love unfailing; with compassion touch the ailing.
3. Sacrificing? I would bring it. But I offer broken spirit.

Cast me not, Lord, from your presence; Holy Spirit, fill my essence.
Wash away, Lord, things destructive and all evil, that I may live.
I am yours, Lord, for the taking. Heal this old heart; it is breaking.

Text: Rusty Edwards, based on Psalm 51
Music: TRYGGARE KAN INGEN VARA, LM; Swedish folk tune
Text © 1999 Augsburg Fortress

17   Here and Now God

1. Here and Now God, the God of beginnings,
   come, Holy Spirit, much closer to me;
   Pentecost Wind, and Breath of the living,
   you have the power to set my heart free.

2. You bear the gifts that wash and enlighten,
   you make me holy with faith eyes to see.
   Here and now, God of all new beginnings,
   come, Holy Spirit, much closer to me.

Text: Rusty Edwards
Music: PENTECOST WIND, 10 10 10 10 D; Linda Cable Shute
© 1999 Augsburg Fortress

Let this season be
Springtime of the Soul

19

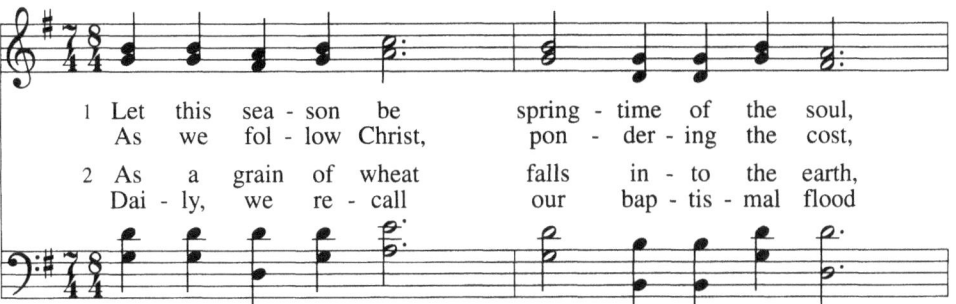

1 Let this sea - son be spring - time of the soul,
  As we fol - low Christ, pon - der - ing the cost,
2 As a grain of wheat falls in - to the earth,
  Dai - ly, we re - call our bap - tis - mal flood

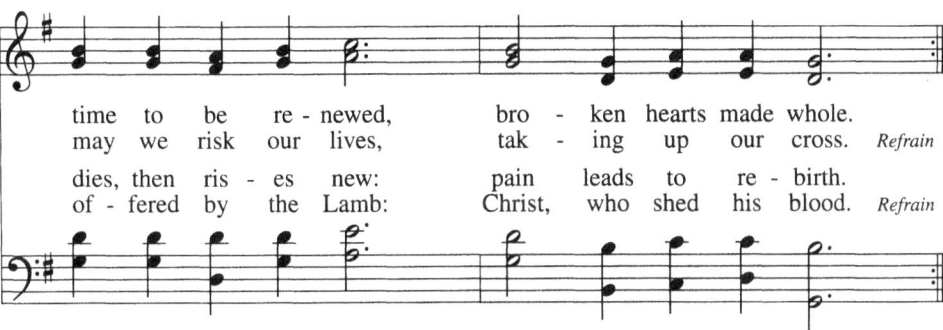

time to be re - newed, bro - ken hearts made whole.
may we risk our lives, tak - ing up our cross. *Refrain*
dies, then ris - es new: pain leads to re - birth.
of - fered by the Lamb: Christ, who shed his blood. *Refrain*

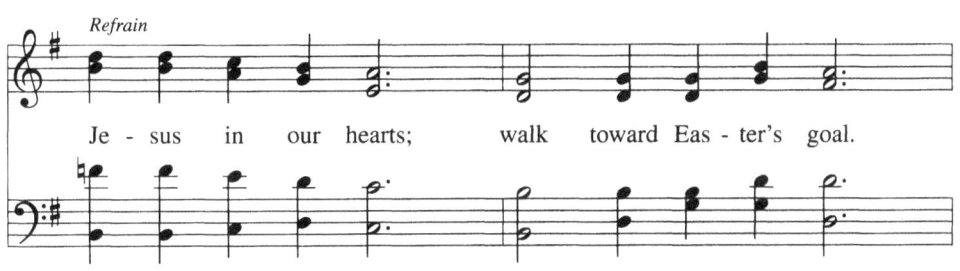

Refrain
Je - sus in our hearts; walk toward Eas - ter's goal.

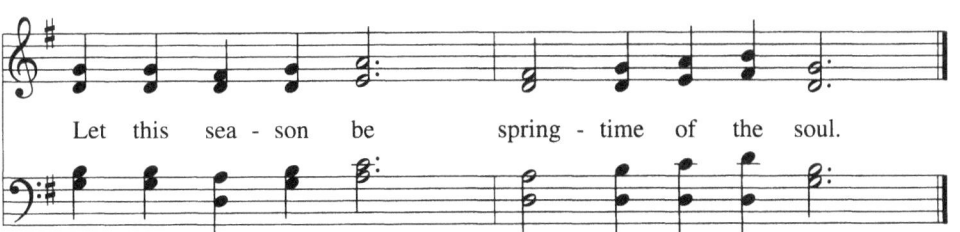

Let this sea - son be spring - time of the soul.

Text: Rusty Edwards
Music: SPRINGTIME OF THE SOUL, 5 5 5 5 D and refrain; Rusty Edwards
© 1999 Augsburg Fortress

20 Like a rose at peak of blooming

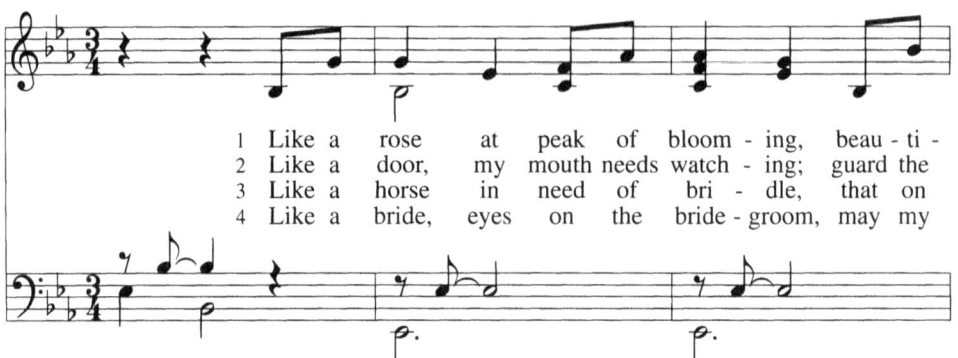

1 Like a rose at peak of bloom-ing, beau-ti-
2 Like a door, my mouth needs watch-ing; guard the
3 Like a horse in need of bri-dle, that on
4 Like a bride, eyes on the bride-groom, may my

ful to smell and view, or the scent of eve-ning
words my lips might say. Draw my heart to good, not
paths it may be led, let me see re-buke as
gaze be fixed on you. Keep me safe from traps set

in-cense, may my prayers un-fold to you.
e-vil, from the morn to end of day.
kind-ness, cool-ing oil up-on my head.
wait-ing; may my steps be right and true.

Text: Rusty Edwards, based on Psalm 141
Music: THE ROSE, 8 7 8 7; Susanne Bågenfelt
© 1999 Augsburg Fortress

Little one, born to bring us such love

1 Lit - tle one, born to bring us such love, lit - tle one,
2 Hold us, dear God, as this child is held close to your
3 Can - cel our an - ger, tem - per our tears, ban - ish the
4 Ho - ly and ten - der Spir - it of God, you do not

wrapped a - round by our prayer, giv - en and tak - en,
heart, to com - fort our pain; we, too, are chil - dren,
blame we keep to our cost, tell us the words we
leave us strug - gling a - lone; sleep - ing or wak - ing,

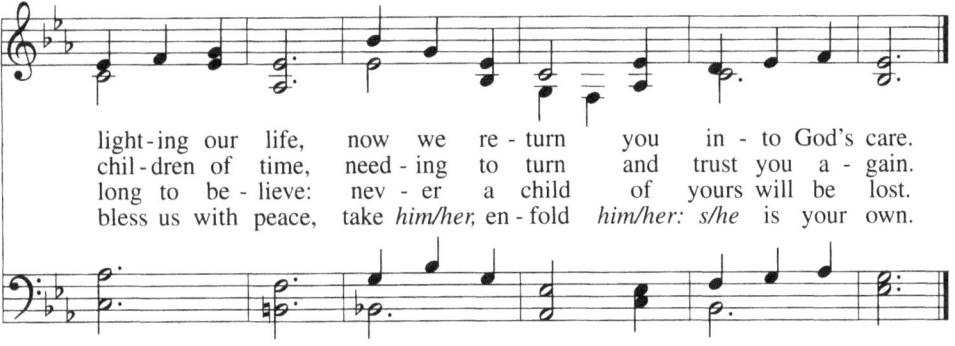

light - ing our life, now we re - turn you in - to God's care.
chil - dren of time, need - ing to turn and trust you a - gain.
long to be - lieve: nev - er a child of yours will be lost.
bless us with peace, take *him/her*, en - fold *him/her*: s/he is your own.

Text: Shirley Erena Murray
Music: CEARA, 9999; Rusty Edwards
© 1999 Hope Publishing Co.

May you look beyond seeing

Text: Rusty Edwards
Music: LOREN, 7676; Linda Cable Shute
© 1999 Augsburg Fortress

Text: Susanne Bågenfelt; English version Rusty Edwards; based on Psalm 23
Music: My Good Shepherd, 7 6 7 5 D and refrain; Susanne Bågenfelt
© 1999 Augsburg Fortress

My joy was shared

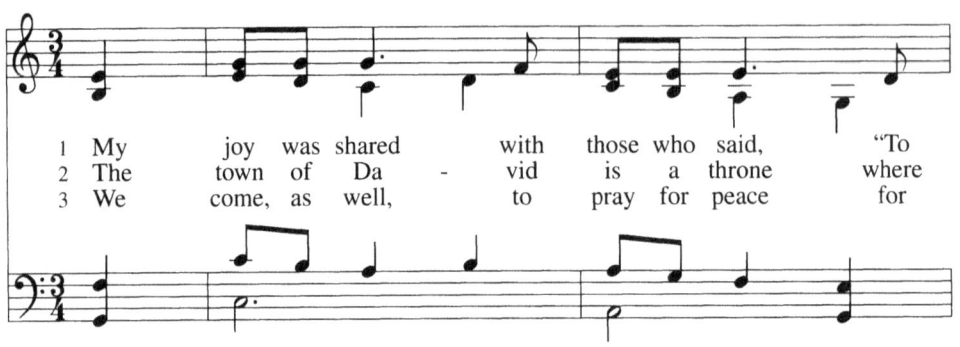

1 My joy was shared with those who said, "To God's house we shall climb." Our feet will stand beside the gates of God's Jerusalem.

2 The town of David is a throne where all the tribes shall go in tribute to the Name of names, according to the law.

3 We come, as well, to pray for peace for fam-'ly, foes, and friends: all children of the one in whom all life begins and ends.

Text: Rusty Edwards, based on Psalm 122
Music: CHEAHA MOUNTAIN, CM; Rusty Edwards
© 1999 Augsburg Fortress

26 My soul finds rest in God alone

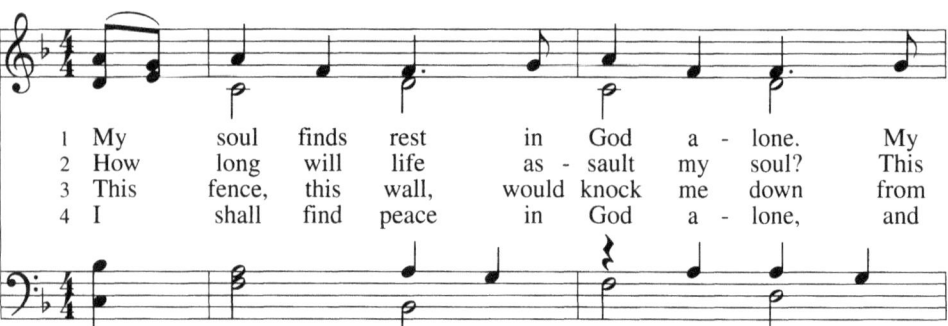

1 My soul finds rest in God a-lone. My
2 How long will life as-sault my soul? This
3 This fence, this wall, would knock me down from
4 I shall find peace in God a-lone, and

heart does God a-wak-en. A rock, a shel-ter
ill-built fence is break-ing, a wall a-bout to
where I have been stand-ing. Their words, they bless. Their
will not be for-sak-en. A rock, a shel-ter

is my God. I nev-er will be shak-en.
fall on me. A farce, my life is mak-ing.
hearts, they curse. The pain is in the land-ing.
is my God. I nev-er will be shak-en.

Text: Rusty Edwards, based on Psalm 62
Music: GODSHELTER, 8787; Jane Marshall
© 1999 Augsburg Fortress

Now is the time to sing with joy! 27

1 Now is the time to sing with joy! Pro-claim the
2 Now say to God, "How strong you are: be - yond all
3 If we had lived to cher - ish sin, God could have
4 So come and see all God has blessed, hills, riv - ers,

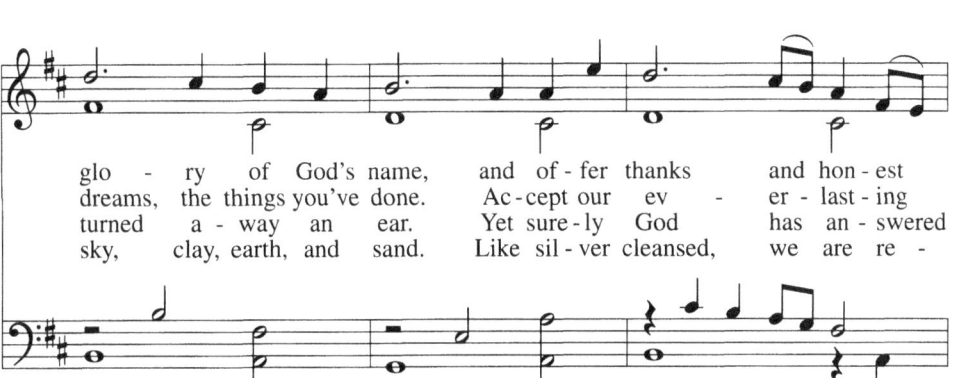

glo - ry of God's name, and of - fer thanks and hon - est
dreams, the things you've done. Ac-cept our ev - er - last - ing
turned a - way an ear. Yet sure - ly God has an - swered
sky, clay, earth, and sand. Like sil - ver cleansed, we are re -

praise, for this is why we came.
praise, for we have just be - gun."
prayer. Each word we say, God hears.
fined; all good is from God's hand.

Text: Rusty Edwards, based on Psalm 66
Music: HIGHLANDS, 8886; Linda Cable Shute
© 1999 Augsburg Fortress

Out of the depths you lifted me

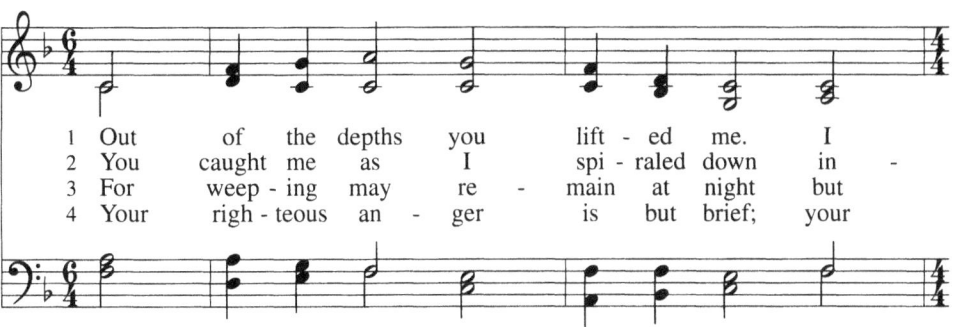
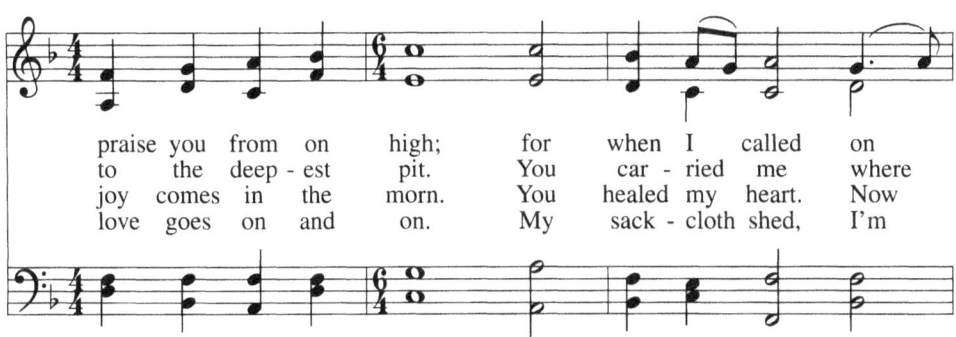
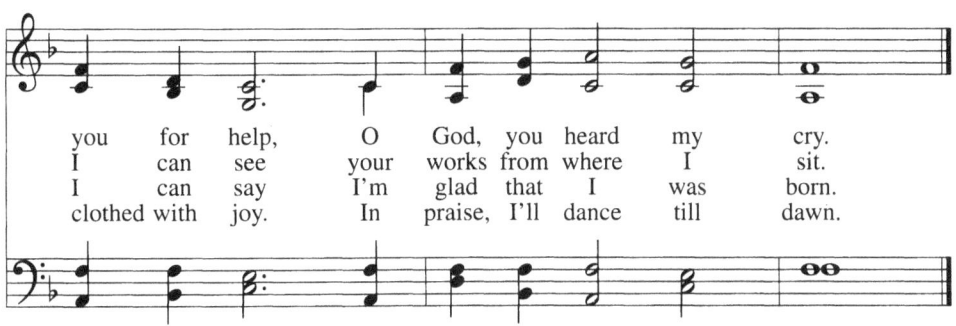

1. Out of the depths you lift-ed me. I praise you from on high; for when I called on you for help, O God, you heard my cry.
2. You caught me as I spi-raled down in-to the deep-est pit. You car-ried me where I can see your works from where I sit.
3. For weep-ing may re-main at night but joy comes in the morn. You healed my heart. Now I can say I'm glad that I was born.
4. Your righ-teous an-ger is but brief; your love goes on and on. My sack-cloth shed, I'm clothed with joy. In praise, I'll dance till dawn.

Text: Rusty Edwards, based on Psalm 30
Music: TWENTY-FOURTH, CM; Lucius Chapin
Text © 1999 Augsburg Fortress

stay with you al - ways. You are my Lord.
songs of grate-ful joy: "You are my Lord."
stay with you al - ways. You are my Lord.

Optional interlude

Text: Richard Drexler and Rusty Edwards
Music: SIMPLE SONG, 10 8 8 5 10 8 7 4; Richard Drexler and Rusty Edwards
© 1999 Augsburg Fortress

Enter, Holy Spirit! 31

1 En - ter, Ho - ly Spir - it! Come, en - joy our prais - es.
2 Je - sus, be a - mong us. Bless us with your pres - ence.
3 Mer - ci - ful Cre - a - tor, come, let us a - dore you.

Spir - it, you are wel - come here and now.
Je - sus, you are wel - come here and now.
Stay, for you are wel - come here and now.

Text: Rusty Edwards
Music: ORTHODOX KYRIE, 6 6 9; Russian Orthodox
Text © 1999 Augsburg Fortress

Text: Rusty Edwards
Music: ONE SACRED MOMENT, 9 8 7 7 and refrain; Linda Cable Shute
© 1999 Augsburg Fortress

Praise the One who breaks the darkness 34

1 Praise the One who breaks the dark-ness with a lib-er-at-ing light;
2 Praise the One who blessed the chil-dren with a strong yet gen-tle word;
3 Praise the one true love in-car-nate: Christ, who suf-fered in our place;

praise the One who frees the pris-'ners, turn-ing blind-ness in-to sight.
praise the One who drove out de-mons with a pierc-ing, two-edged sword.
Je-sus died and rose for man-y that we may know God by grace.

Praise the One who preached the gos-pel, heal-ing ev-'ry dread dis-ease,
Praise the One who brings cool wa-ter to the des-ert's burn-ing sand;
Let us sing for joy and glad-ness, see-ing what our God has done.

calm-ing storms and feed-ing thou-sands with the ver-y bread of peace.
from this well comes liv-ing wa-ter quench-ing thirst in ev-'ry land.
Praise the one re-deem-ing glo-ry; praise the One who makes us one.

Text: Rusty Edwards
Music: NETTLETON, 8 7 8 7 D; Wyeth's *Repository of Sacred Music*, Part II
Text © 1986 Hope Publishing Co.

35   Search my heart, Jesus

1. Search my heart, Jesus, and teach me your ways.
   You know my thoughts and the course of my days.
2. If I would flee from you, where would I hide?
   In ev-'ry heart-ache, you stand by my side.
3. Deep in the darkness of my mother's womb,
   you formed me, and I continue to bloom.
4. Precious are your thoughts, my Jesus, to me.
   They would outnumber the sands of the sea.
5. If I could rise on the wings of the dawn,
   if you go with me, then I will fly on!

Refrain
For your love is true. Jesus, I love you. Never part; O Lord, search my

Text: Rusty Edwards, based on Psalm 139
Music: KIMBERLY MICHELLE, 5 5 5 5 and refrain; Rusty Edwards
© 1999 Augsburg Fortress

36 Spirit Wind

1. Spirit Wind, hear my plea; holy breeze, blow through me.
2. Make my life dead to sin, that you may enter in.
3. Lord, anoint me some way; make my heart fresh today.
4. Sacred Light, through me shine; take your truth, make it mine.

*may be sung as a round

Text: Rusty Edwards
Music: COGGIN, 3 3 3 3; Benjamin Edwards
© 1999 Augsburg Fortress

37 Send out your light

1. Send out your light as sacred proof, and as its partner, gospel truth. They guide us to your
2. Straight to your altar we shall go, as joy on joy begins to grow. With light and truth to
3. No souls on earth need sorrow now; hope in the one to whom we bow. Joy draws a peace up-

holy hill, close to your home, your heart, your will.
ease the way, we move in praise of you this day.
on each face, as we draw near your per-fect place.

Text: Rusty Edwards, based on Psalm 43
Music: SANDTOWN, LM; Jane Marshall
© 1999 Augsburg Fortress

Stir up your power 38

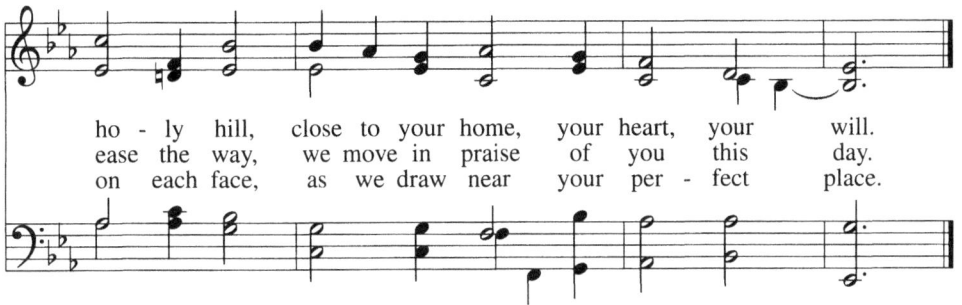

1 Stir up your pow'r, O Lord, and come. A-gain we
2 Is heav-en's mo - ment far or near? And when will
3 We could in - side the church re - main, like dry ground
4 But we must keep hands to the plow; God's time is

pray, "Your will be done." May Ad-vent blue to us fore-
Je - sus re-ap - pear? The com-ing dawn is our de-
watch - ing for the rain. We could de - cide to sit and
both not yet and now. Our faith in - forms what we shall

tell the ech - o of Em-man - u - el.
light in this, the dark-est hour of night.
wait as Je - sus we an - ti - ci - pate.
do. May Christ re - turn and find us true.

Text: Rusty Edwards
Music: ADVENT BLUE, LM; Linda Cable Shute
© 1999 Augsburg Fortress

39   The walls will echo praises

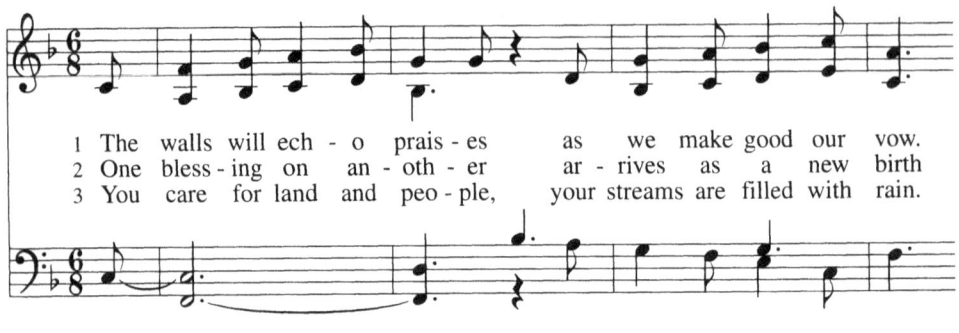

1 The walls will ech-o prais-es   as we make good our vow.
2 One bless-ing on an-oth-er   ar-rives as a new birth
3 You care for land and peo-ple,   your streams are filled with rain.

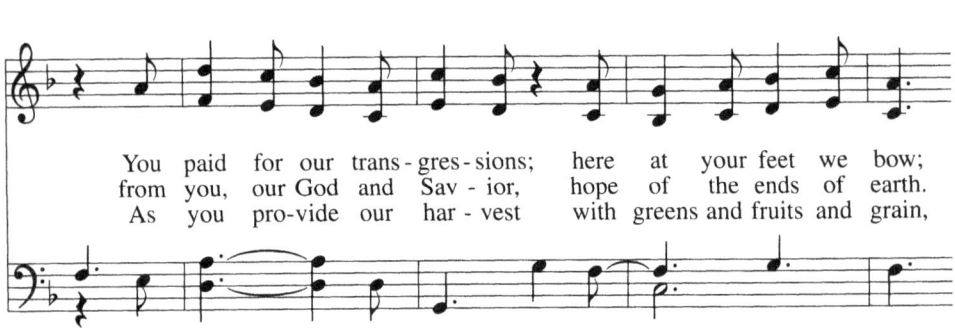

You paid for our trans-gres-sions;   here at your feet we bow;
from you, our God and Sav-ior,   hope of the ends of earth.
As you pro-vide our har-vest   with greens and fruits and grain,

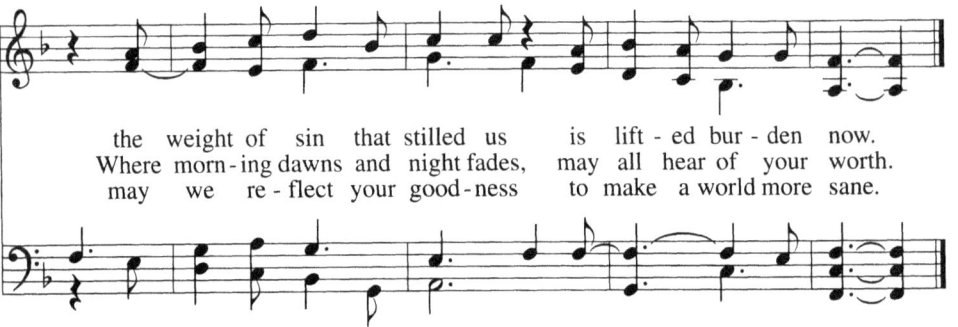

the weight of sin that stilled us   is lift-ed bur-den now.
Where morn-ing dawns and night fades,   may all hear of your worth.
may we re-flect your good-ness   to make a world more sane.

Text: Rusty Edwards, based on Psalm 65
Music: BOUNTY AND PRAISE, 7 6 7 6 7 6; Linda Cable Shute
© 1999 Augsburg Fortress

To a maid engaged to Joseph 40

Text: Gracia Grindal
Music: ANNUNCIATION, 767676; Rusty Edwards
© 1984 Hope Publishing Co.

Text: Rusty Edwards and Susanne Bågenfelt
Music: I Believe, LM and refrain; Susanne Bågenfelt
© 1999 Augsburg Fortress

Upon a donkey's colt you ride

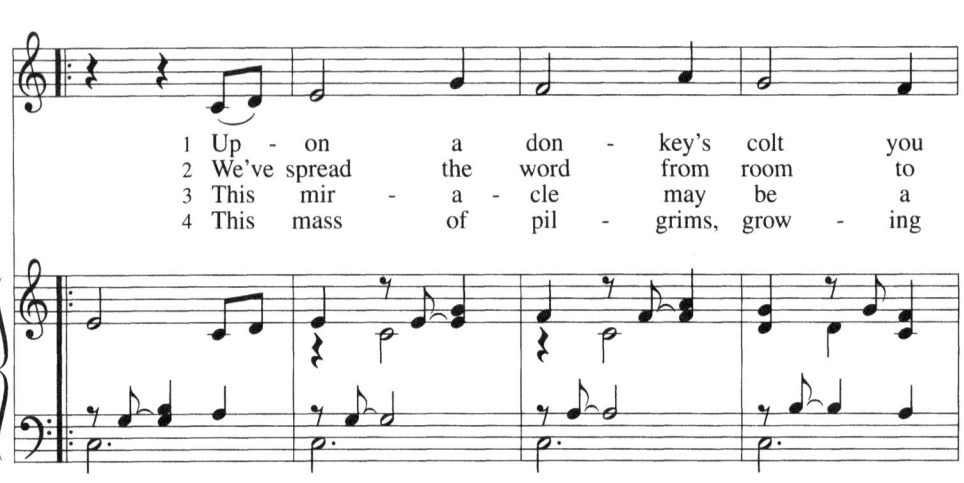

1. Up - on a don - key's colt you
2. We've spread the word from room to
3. This mir - a - cle may be a
4. This mass of pil - grims, grow - ing

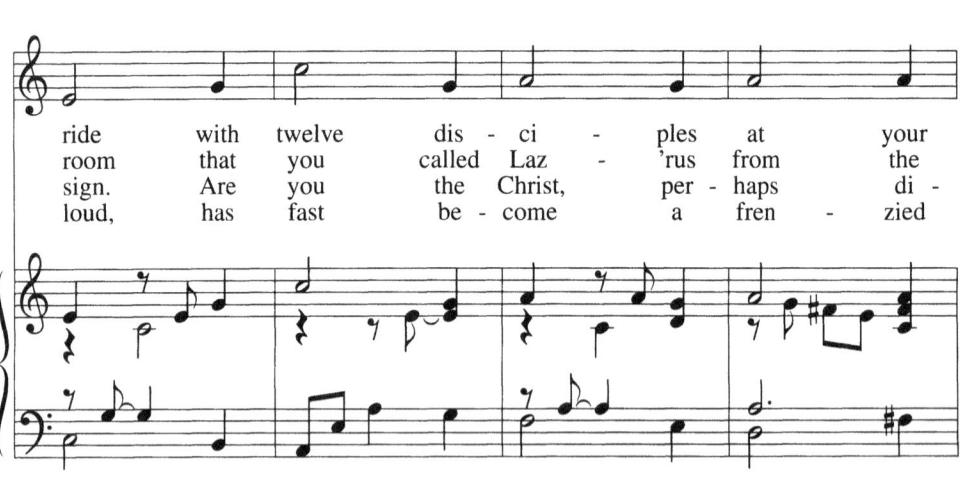

ride with twelve dis - ci - ples at your
room that you called Laz - 'rus from the
sign. Are you the Christ, per - haps di -
loud, has fast be - come a fren - zied

Text: Rusty Edwards
Music: LINEA, L M; Susanne Bågenfelt
© 1999 Augsburg Fortress

43. We all are one in mission

1. We all are one in mission; we all are one in call,
our varied gifts united by Christ, the Lord of all.
A single, great commission compels us from above
to touch the lives of others with God's surprising grace,
so every folk and nation may feel God's warm embrace.

2. We all are called to service, to witness in God's name.
Our ministries are diff'rent; our purpose is the same:
to plan and work together that all may know Christ's love.

3. We all behold one vision, a stark reality:
the author of salvation was nailed upon a tree.
Yet resurrected Justice gives rise that we may share
free reconciliation and hope amid despair.

4. Now let us be united and let our song be heard.
Now let us be a vessel for God's redeeming Word.
We all are one in mission; we all are one in call,
our varied gifts united by Christ, the Lord of all.

Text: Rusty Edwards
Music: ACCORD, 7 6 7 6 D; Dale Wood
Text © 1986 Hope Publishing Co.
Music © 1992 Dale Wood

We lift our eyes   44

1 We lift our eyes to the hills; our God will not slum-ber nor sleep. And
2 We lift our eyes to the hills, for God is our shade, left and right. The
3 We lift our eyes to the hills; our God will keep harm from our door. God

when we climb, we will not stum-ble, for God our Lord will safe-keep.
sun will not harm us at mid-day, nor will the moon in the night.
watch-es our com-ing and go-ing both now and for-ev-er-more.

Text: Rusty Edwards, based on Psalm 121
Music: INDAQUOIA, 7 8 9 7 and refrain; LaJuana Fiester
© 1999 Augsburg Fortress

45 Where two or more are gathered

1 Where two or more are gathered in Jesus' holy name,
a prayer will soon be answered and life is not the same.
The asking we are given at first, to us, seems odd;
not so, if we remember, "Seek first the realm of God."

2 When we begin our praying with selfishness or greed,
we soon will be reminded, God gives us what we need;
not ev-'ry whim or fancy, nor ev-'ry vain desire,
not things that spoil or harm us, but what our lives require.

3 Don't worry for tomorrow, about the clothes we wear,
what food will be provided, or other earthly care,
for God knows that we need them and surely will provide.
Seek first the realm of Jesus. Let God be glorified.

Text: Rusty Edwards
Music: CONSIDER THE LILIES, 7676 D; Linda Cable Shute
© 1999 Augsburg Fortress

Topics and themes

Advent
38 Stir up your power
40 To a maid engaged to Joseph
Affirmation of Baptism
17 Here and Now God
Arts and music
14 Hallelujah! Sing to our God
Ascension
6 Clap your hands! Shout for joy!
15 He is Lord
33 Praise, praise! You are my rock
Ash Wednesday
16 Heal this old heart
Assurance
4 By grace we have been saved
5 Cast your every care on me
18 I will draw you near me
23 My good shepherd is the Lord
25 My light and my salvation
26 My soul finds rest in God alone
29 Out of the depths you lifted me
44 We lift our eyes
Children, Songs for
7 Come, little children
36 Spirit Wind
Christ the King/Reign of Christ
15 He is Lord
Christmas
7 Come, little children
32 One sacred moment
Church
17 Here and Now God
Comfort, Rest
18 I will draw you near me
23 My good shepherd is the Lord
26 My soul finds rest in God alone
29 Out of the depths you lifted me
35 Search my heart, Jesus
44 We lift our eyes
Commitment
43 We all are one in mission
Community in Christ
11 Friends
43 We all are one in mission
Confession
16 Heal this old heart
Creation
1 As sunshine to a garden
13 God recycles, reconciles us

Daily Life
8 Feed my lambs
9 For everything there is a time
22 May you look beyond seeing
30 O Lord, I worship you
43 We all are one in mission
Death of a child
21 Little one, born to bring us such love
Discipleship
8 Feed my lambs
19 Let this season be
28 Now it is evening
Easter
3 Bride and bridegroom
15 He is Lord
23 My good shepherd is the Lord
34 Praise the One who breaks the darkness
33 Praise, praise! You are my rock
Epiphany
37 Send out your light
41 There's a light in the world
43 We all are one in mission
Evening
20 Like a rose at peak of blooming
28 Now it is evening
44 We lift our eyes
Faith
4 By grace we have been saved
10 For God so loved the world
17 Here and Now God
25 My light and my salvation
38 Stir up your power
44 We lift our eyes
Forgiveness
10 For God so loved the world
13 God recycles, reconciles us
16 Heal this old heart
39 The walls will echo praises
Friendship
11 Friends
Gathering
31 Enter, Holy Spirit!
14 Hallelujah! Sing to our God
17 Here and Now God
18 I will draw you near me
24 My joy was shared
27 Now is the time to sing with joy!
37 Send out your light

Grace
4 By grace we have been saved
17 Here and Now God
34 Praise the One who breaks the darkness
Guidance
5 Cast your every care on me
20 Like a rose at peak of blooming
23 My good shepherd is the Lord
35 Search my heart, Jesus
36 Spirit Wind
Healing
2 Be a searchlight
5 Cast your every care on me
9 For everything there is a time
13 God recycles, reconciles us
16 Heal this old heart
18 I will draw you near me
19 Let this season be
29 Out of the depths you lifted me
34 Praise the One who breaks the darkness
33 Praise, praise! You are my rock
Heaven, Eternal Life
10 For God so loved the world
21 Little one, born to bring us such love
23 My good shepherd is the Lord
Holy Baptism
10 For God so loved the world
12 God of all new birth
17 Here and Now God
22 May you look beyond seeing
Holy Communion
33 Praise, praise! You are my rock
Holy Spirit
31 Enter, Holy Spirit!
17 Here and Now God
36 Spirit Wind
Holy Trinity, The
31 Enter, Holy Spirit!
Hope
5 Cast your every care on me
10 For God so loved the world
23 My good shepherd is the Lord
Incarnation
32 One sacred moment
34 Praise the One who breaks the darkness
40 To a maid engaged to Joseph

Joy
- 6 Clap your hands! Shout for joy!
- 14 Hallelujah! Sing to our God
- 24 My joy was shared
- 27 Now is the time to sing with joy!
- 37 Send out your light

Kingdom of God/Reign of God
- 6 Clap your hands! Shout for joy!
- 45 Where two or more are gathered

Last Times
- 3 Bride and bridegroom

Lent
- 1 As sunshine to a garden
- 4 By grace we have been saved
- 10 For God so loved the world
- 16 Heal this old heart
- 19 Let this season be
- 33 Praise, praise! You are my rock

Light
- 25 My light and my salvation
- 28 Now it is evening
- 32 One sacred moment
- 34 Praise the One who breaks the darkness
- 37 Send out your light
- 41 There's a light in the world

Love
- 1 As sunshine to a garden
- 4 By grace we have been saved
- 11 Friends
- 29 Out of the depths you lifted me

Ministry
- 2 Be a searchlight
- 8 Feed my lambs
- 28 Now it is evening

Mission
- 2 Be a searchlight
- 8 Feed my lambs
- 38 Stir up your power
- 39 The walls will echo praises
- 41 There's a light in the world
- 43 We all are one in mission

Offertory
- 30 O Lord, I worship you

Peace
- 23 My good shepherd is the Lord
- 24 My joy was shared
- 26 My soul finds rest in God alone
- 37 Send out your light

Pentecost
- 31 Enter, Holy Spirit!
- 17 Here and Now God
- 36 Spirit Wind

Praise, Adoration
- 3 Bride and bridegroom
- 6 Clap your hands! Shout for joy!
- 14 Hallelujah! Sing to our God
- 27 Now is the time to sing with joy!
- 30 O Lord, I worship you
- 29 Out of the depths you lifted me
- 34 Praise the One who breaks the darkness
- 33 Praise, praise! You are my rock
- 46 With highest praise

Prayer
- 16 Heal this old heart
- 20 Like a rose at peak of blooming
- 24 My joy was shared
- 25 My light and my salvation
- 35 Search my heart, Jesus
- 36 Spirit Wind
- 45 Where two or more are gathered

Reconciliation
- 9 For everything there is a time
- 13 God recycles, reconciles us
- 16 Heal this old heart
- 19 Let this season be
- 24 My joy was shared

Reformation Day
- 4 By grace we have been saved
- 43 We all are one in mission

Repentance
- 19 Let this season be

Salvation
- 10 For God so loved the world

Sending
- 22 May you look beyond seeing
- 43 We all are one in mission

Service
- 2 Be a searchlight
- 8 Feed my lambs
- 28 Now it is evening
- 38 Stir up your power
- 39 The walls will echo praises
- 43 We all are one in mission

Society
- 2 Be a searchlight
- 28 Now it is evening

Stewardship
- 2 Be a searchlight
- 13 God recycles, reconciles us
- 45 Where two or more are gathered

Stillbirth
- 21 Little one, born to bring us such love

Suffering
- 5 Cast your every care on me

Sunday of the Passion
- 15 He is Lord
- 42 Upon a donkey's colt you ride

Thanksgiving
- 27 Now is the time to sing with joy!
- 29 Out of the depths you lifted me
- 39 The walls will echo praises
- 46 With highest praise

Trust
- 5 Cast your every care on me
- 23 My good shepherd is the Lord
- 25 My light and my salvation
- 26 My soul finds rest in God alone
- 33 Praise, praise! You are my rock
- 44 We lift our eyes
- 45 Where two or more are gathered

Unity
- 24 My joy was shared
- 34 Praise the One who breaks the darkness
- 43 We all are one in mission

Watchfulness
- 38 Stir up your power

Witness
- 8 Feed my lambs
- 15 He is Lord
- 37 Send out your light
- 43 We all are one in mission

Word, The
- 1 As sunshine to a garden

Worship
- 24 My joy was shared
- 27 Now is the time to sing with joy!
- 39 The walls will echo praises
- 46 With highest praise

Scripture references

Genesis
1:26-30	13	God recycles, reconciles us

Psalms
23	23	My good shepherd is the Lord
27	25	My light and my salvation
30	29	Out of the depths you lifted me
43	37	Send out your light
47	6	Clap your hands! Shout for joy!
51	16	Heal this old heart
62	26	My soul finds rest in God alone
65	39	The walls will echo praises
66	27	Now is the time to sing with joy!
78:15-16	33	Praise, praise! You are my rock
111	46	With highest praise
121	44	We lift our eyes
122	24	My joy was shared
139	35	Search my heart, Jesus
141	20	Like a rose at peak of blooming
149	14	Hallelujah! Sing to our God

Ecclesiastes
3:1-8	9	For everything there is a time

Isaiah
43:1	12	God of all new birth
55:10-11	1	As sunshine to a garden
58:11	1	As sunshine to a garden

Jeremiah
31:1-14	18	I will draw you near me

Matthew
4:16	34	Praise the One who breaks the darkness
5:14	2	Be a searchlight
6:28-33	45	Where two or more are gathered
7:7-8	45	Where two or more are gathered
7:16	1	As sunshine to a garden
11:28-30	5	Cast your every care on me
16:24-25	19	Let this season be
18:19-20	45	Where two or more are gathered
21:1-11	42	Upon a donkey's colt you ride
25:31-40	2	Be a searchlight
25:31-40	8	Feed my lambs
25:31-40	28	Now it is evening

Mark
8:34-35	19	Let this season be
11:1-10	42	Upon a donkey's colt you ride

Luke
1:26-38	40	To a maid engaged to Joseph
2:1-20	7	Come, little children
2:15-20	32	One sacred moment
9:23-24	19	Let this season be
10:25-37	28	Now it is evening
15:3-10	8	Feed my lambs
19:28-38	42	Upon a donkey's colt you ride

John
1:4-5	41	There's a light in the world
3:1-17	10	For God so loved the world
3:16	41	There's a light in the world
8:12	28	Now it is evening
8:12	41	There's a light in the world
12:12-19	42	Upon a donkey's colt you ride
12:24	19	Let this season be
12:46	41	There's a light in the world
15:13	11	Friends
21:15-19	8	Feed my lambs

Acts
1:9-11	33	Praise, praise! You are my rock

Romans
3:21-26	4	By grace we have been saved
10:15	4	By grace we have been saved

1 Corinthians
2:12-13	17	Here and Now God
12	43	We all are one in mission
12:3	17	Here and Now God

Ephesians
2:8	4	By grace we have been saved
4:1-13	43	We all are one in mission

Philippians
2:5-11	15	He is Lord

2 Thessalonians
2:14	17	Here and Now God

1 Peter
4:10	43	We all are one in mission
5:7	5	Cast your every care on me

Revelation
19:6-8	3	Bride and bridegroom
21:23	41	There's a light in the world
22:5	41	There's a light in the world
22:16	3	Bride and bridegroom

Tunes—alphabetical

43	Accord	11	Faithful Richard	9	Narvesen
38	Advent Blue			34	Nettleton
25	Amicalola Falls	26	Godshelter		
40	Annunciation			4	Oh, How I Love Jesus
14	Atlanta	15	He Is Lord	5	One Less Tear
		46	Highest Praise	32	One Sacred Moment
2	Bob and Jerry	27	Highlands	31	Orthodox Kyrie
39	Bounty and Praise	7	Howard		
28	Bozeman			17	Pentecost Wind
12	Bunessan	41	I Believe		
		44	Indaquoia	37	Sandtown
21	Ceara			30	Simple Song
24	Cheaha Mountain	6	Kennesaw Mountain	19	Springtime of the Soul
36	Coggin	35	Kimberly Michelle		
45	Consider the Lilies			1	The Garden Song
		3	Lamb's Wedding	20	The Rose
18	Draw Near	42	Linea	10	Three Sixteen
		22	Loren	16	Tryggare kan ingen vara
13	Earth Day Hymn			29	Twenty-fourth
		8	Mary Lou		
		23	My Good Shepherd	33	Zachary Woods Rock

Tunes—metrical

C M
   Cheaha Mountain 24
   Twenty-fourth 29
C M and refrain
   Oh, How I Love Jesus 4
L M
   Advent Blue 38
   Highest Praise 46
   Linea 42
   Narvesen 9
   Sandtown 37
   Tryggare kan ingen vara 16
L M and refrain
   I Believe 41
3 3 3 3
   Coggin 36
5 5 5 4 D
   Bunessan 12
   Bozeman 28
5 5 5 5 and refrain
   Kimberly Michelle 35
5 5 5 5 D and refrain
   Springtime of the Soul 19
6 5 6 5 D
   Draw Near 18
6 6 8 8 8
   Zachary Woods Rock 33

6 6 9
   Orthodox Kyrie 31
6 7 6 7
   Kennesaw Mountain 6
6 11 10 6
   He Is Lord 15
7 6 7 5 D and refrain
   My Good Shepherd 23
7 6 7 6
   Loren 22
   The Garden Song 1
7 6 7 6 7 6
   Annunciation 40
   Bounty and Praise 39
7 6 7 6 D
   Accord 43
   Amicalola Falls 25
   Consider the Lilies 45
7 7 7 7
   One Less Tear 5
7 8 9 7 and refrain
   Indaquoia 44
8 5 9 5 and refrain
   Three Sixteen 10
8 6 8 6 6
   Atlanta 14

8 7 8 7
   Bob and Jerry 2
   Earth Day Hymn 13
   Godshelter 26
   The Rose 20
8 7 8 7 D
   Nettleton 34
8 8 8 6
   Highlands 27
8 8 8 7 and refrain
   Lamb's Wedding 3
9 8 7 7 and refrain
   One Sacred Moment 32
9 9 9 9
   Ceara 21
9 11 9 11
   Mary Lou 8
10 8 8 5 10 8 7 4
   Simple Song 30
10 10 10 10 D
   Pentecost Wind 17
11 10 11 10
   Howard 7
11 11 11 12
   Faithful Richard 11

Contributors and sources

Bågenfelt, Susanne 1, 3, 20, 23, 41, 42
Bisbee, B. Wayne 12
Brokering, Herbert F. 7, 33
Chapin, Lucius 29
Drexler, Richard 30
Edwards, Benjamin 36
Fiester, LaJuana 44
Gaelic traditional 12
Grindal, Gracia 40
Marshall, Jane 13, 14, 26, 37
Murray, Shirley Erena 21
North American traditional 4
Pratt Green, Fred 28
Russian Orthodox 31
Schmit, Clayton J. 11
Shute, Linda Cable 6, 17, 18, 22, 27, 32, 38, 39, 45, 46
Sterling, Robert 7
Swedish folk tune 16
Traditional 15
Whitfield, Frederick 4
Wood, Dale 43
Wyeth's *Repository of Sacred Music*, Part II 34

First lines and titles

1 As sunshine to a garden
2 Be a searchlight
3 Bride and bridegroom
4 By grace we have been saved
5 Cast your every care on me
6 Clap your hands! Shout for joy!
7 Come, little children
31 Enter, Holy Spirit!
8 Feed my lambs
9 For everything there is a time
10 For God so loved the world
11 Friends
12 God of all new birth
13 God recycles, reconciles us
14 Hallelujah! Sing to our God
15 He is Lord
16 Heal this old heart
17 Here and Now God
18 I will draw you near me
19 Let this season be
20 Like a rose at peak of blooming
21 Little one, born to bring us such love
22 May you look beyond seeing
23 My good shepherd is the Lord
24 My joy was shared
25 My light and my salvation
26 My soul finds rest in God alone
27 Now is the time to sing with joy!
28 Now it is evening
30 O Lord, I worship you
32 One sacred moment
29 Out of the depths you lifted me
33 Praise, praise! You are my rock
34 Praise the One who breaks the darkness
35 Search my heart, Jesus
37 Send out your light
30 *Simple Song*
36 Spirit Wind
19 *Springtime of the Soul*
38 Stir up your power
1 *The Garden Song*
39 The walls will echo praises
41 There's a light in the world
40 To a maid engaged to Joseph
42 Upon a donkey's colt you ride
43 We all are one in mission
44 We lift our eyes
45 Where two or more are gathered
46 With highest praise

www.ingramcontent.com/pod-product-compliance
Lightning Source LLC
Chambersburg PA
CBHW051958290426
44110CB00015B/2290